BIOGRAPHY AS HISTORY

Men and Movements in Europe since 1500

By CHARLES F. MULLETT
University of Missouri

Publication Number 49

SERVICE CENTER FOR TEACHERS OF HISTORY
A Service of the American Historical Association

THE MACMILLAN COMPANY

60 Fifth Avenue, New York

The American Historical Association, because of its continuing interest in the teaching of history in the schools of the United States, has established the Service Center for Teachers of History in an effort to offer constructive assistance in solving some of the problems which today beset the classroom teacher. One of the programs being sponsored by the Service Center is the preparation of a series of pamphlets, each containing a concise summary of publications reflecting recent research and new interpretations in a particular field of history.

Since many secondary school teachers have neither the time nor opportunity to read widely in monographic literature, these pamphlets have been specifically designed to meet classroom teachers' needs. Each pamphlet purports to bring the reader abreast of current interpretations and significant writings in a specific field of historical study. Our aim is, in short, to help the teachers help themselves by keeping up to date in their fields of interest. It is our sincere hope that this will materially benefit the teacher and thereby contribute to the enrichment of classroom instruction. The extent to which the project is successful will be measured by the degree to which the regrettable gap between the teacher of history in the school and the specialist in historical research is narrowed.

WALTER RUNDELL, JR.

BIOGRAPHY AS HISTORY: MEN AND MOVEMENTS IN EUROPE SINCE 1500

By CHARLES F. MULLETT

University of Missouri

A Publication of the American Historical Association's
SERVICE CENTER FOR TEACHERS OF HISTORY
400 A Street, S. E., Washington 3, D. C.

THE MACMILLAN COMPANY, NEW YORK
COLLIER-MACMILLAN LIMITED, LONDON

First Printing

Library of Congress catalog card number: 63–9222
The Macmillan Company, New York
Collier-Macmillan Canada, Ltd., Toronto, Ontario
DIVISIONS OF THE CROWELL-COLLIER PUBLISHING COMPANY

Printed in the United States of America

COMMITTEE ON TEACHING OF THE

AMERICAN HISTORICAL ASSOCIATION

A Word to the Reader

The following pages first estimate the value and sketch the development of biography and, secondly, relate men to events and tendencies. I have chosen my subjects arbitrarily, not seeking completeness or perfection, for in many instances the availability of materials and familiarity with subject matter have shaped my choices. Throughout I have tried to select men important for their time as well as for years to come, men who were typical but not stereotypical. Doubtless other subjects would have better satisfied many readers; but, ever clutching at a pedagogical straw, let me suggest that some value may accrue from two or three assignments. Propose one debate on better choices, another on why some men have, and others have not, got biographies, a third on what men of today are likely to be remembered twenty, fifty, two hundred years hence, and why. Trace the *reputation* of a well known personality through different periods of the past; account for the contrasting interpretations of such a personality by different authors in the same period. Consider also a calendar of great men for other areas and other periods. Once such projects are attempted the richness of the subject and the problems of choice will be fully appreciated.

Those who teach history should be continually concerned with the task of seeking the solid and the concrete behind the empty and abstract . . . it is on men rather than functions that they should concentrate their attention.

Marc Bloch

Who knows whether the best of men be known? or whether there be not more remarkable persons forgot?

Sir Thomas Browne

History does nothing, it possesses no immense wealth, fights no battles. It is rather *man,* real living *man* who does everything, who possesses and fights.

Karl Marx

1

Biography as History: Men and Movements in Europe Since 1500

By CHARLES F. MULLETT

The Nature of Biography

First and last history is about people, what they do, what they think, what happens to them, and how they influence the world in which they live. No matter the attention to deeds, institutions, and ideas, the historian comes back to the men who performed the deeds, ran the institutions, and conceived the ideas. Without people history is inconceivable; the history of a country, an idea, a policy means the men who built it, or thought it, or carried it through. To describe these men is enormously difficult. The biographer may have too few or too many facts. The evidence is often questionable but he nevertheless has to do the best he can; he tries to give life to what he finds, and perhaps in the process invents when he does not know; he is perpetually trying, sometimes in vain, to find the man within the shell of evidence. Because he risks overrating his subject's importance, he must also recreate the world in which the man lived.

The pioneering biographer, Plutarch, 2000 years ago took his readers into the private lodgings of the hero. It was not always, he said, the greatest achievements that disclosed a person's real character, "but very often an action of small note, a short saying, or a jest." Although some background is desirable, biographers should neither lose the individual in the "times" nor merely append the "times," often "unchewed and crude," nor forget that what illumines one "life" may obscure another. For instance in 1687 James II of England framed religious policies that led to his overthrow, and Isaac Newton produced his *Principia*, but no biographer of Newton should clutter his pages with ecclesiastical inci-

3

dents. Lacking a universal formula, we applaud that biographer who achieves a nice balance between life and times.

Samuel Johnson, no mean biographer himself, esteemed biography "as giving us what comes near to ourselves." A blade of grass, he went on, "is always a blade of grass, whether in one country or another. . . . Men and women are my subjects of inquiry; let us see how they differ from those we have left behind." Too often, he thought, biographers contented themselves with a chronological series of actions which anyone might collect from the public papers whereas they should avoid the "formal and studied narrative, begun with his pedigree, and ended with his funeral." Rather they must attend to the "little circumstances"—family, education, travel, reading, profession, associates—circumstances that explain how a man became what he was and why.

How far may an author stress peculiarities? Certainly not to the extent of creating merely an eccentric. He should mention vices only if these are relevant, though some biographers seem anxious to confect only a tissue of scandal in contrast to works of no greater value written when eulogy was the order of the day. "Better that we know a painter only through his vision or a poet by his song," said Oscar Wilde in words that apply as well to soldiers, statesmen, merchants, and philosophers, "than that the image of a great man should be marred and made mean by the clumsy geniality of good intentions."

Good biography is most enjoyable and instructive, possessing the interest of fiction, accuracy of history, and insight of poetry. Yet it has its pitfalls. The total picture of social change can be distorted by such concentration on an individual that we fail to see the man in relation to his times. Over a century ago the eloquent Thomas Carlyle urged the biographer "to find out the great men, clean the dirt from them and place them on their proper pedestals"; more recently many biographers have exalted men of low degree. Neither objective encompasses the historical value of biography. Great crises thrust greatness upon men and bring forth what otherwise might have lain fallow.

Some periods, some themes profit especially from biography, for instance a new country, an era of rapid social change, a theme newly explored. Here again the writer must beware claiming too much, lest the topic become only a conjunction of selected spectacular personalities. In the history of ideas especially one must attend to those lesser individuals who made the genius possible and his ideas acceptable, even now and again to men who misfired and by so doing pointed the right way. If we consider history the essence of innumerable biographies we must make sure that we include the hewers of wood and drawers of water as well as the captains and the kings.

In the largest sense biography extends to ideas, attitudes, groups— the constant awareness that not only did Napoleon and Lenin do something, that not only did Newton, Rousseau, and Marx conceive something, but that thousands of nameless contemporaries made their deeds and thoughts possible and effective. If we remember the unknown as well as the known, we shall more readily escape the glib attribution of paternity of some idea or institution to one man. The stress here upon ideas is deliberate: biography is not least the history of the human mind. If ever a dreary catalogue of faceless forces glued together with the jargon of the hour does duty for the human drama, history will be one with Queen Anne. The writing of history itself is a testament of biography, for every image of the past is owing to some historian who collected, selected, and related the facts concerning the past. Without him history is an old curiosity shop.

Amid the avalanche of impersonal forces historians sometimes give little thought to men. They have scanted Oliver Cromwell, warts and all, to dispute the rise and/or fall of the gentry, lost Martin Luther in the Protestant ethic and the spirit of capitalism, drowned Napoleon in revolutionary ideology. They might realize that historical labels like last week's slogans serve their term and are replaced by others equally mortal; it is the living individual who captures the imagination. Queen Mary did not burn Protestantism at the stake, she burnt Hugh Latimer. If history becomes anonymous it becomes inevitable, and the individual is cast out with yesterday's refuse. Carlyle's conviction, that great men are profitable company because they open up the very marrow of the past, is graphically illustrated by Alexander the Great as seen through the eyes of W. W. Tarn. Alexander "was one of the supreme fertilizing forces of history. He lifted the civilized world out of one groove and set it in another; he started a new epoch; nothing could again be as it had been." As the instrument of Greek expansion he helped to replace particularism by universalism, he had a splendid dream which men have not yet succeeded in realizing—one world.

The problem of influence is bewildering because we often cannot be sure whether what we are saying is true, no matter how ingeniously we pile up evidence, yet the search must broaden our understanding. The biographer should look at his subject in light and shadow, but never turn him into a bloodless abstraction. The business of the historian and the biographer alike is human affairs and their grounding in the thoughts and feelings of men, or, when and in what way men pursued this or that goal, and with what consequences. Though we may agree with Goethe that "when eras are on the decline all tendencies are subjective, but on the other hand when matters are ripening for a new epoch, all tendencies are objective," to study biography is to appreciate the casual and depreciate inevitably. So many questions can be answered, indeed only be asked, by studying what men have done and with what consequences.

Because biography illustrates so many themes, it has had an informing history in itself. The choice of subjects reflects the environment of the writer. New men first share the scene with old ones and then eclipse them, as more pertinent to the prevailing outlook on that particular segment of the past. On such occasions biographies deal less with an individual than with a stereotype—the saint, the tyrant, the robber baron. The words could as appropriately describe fifty other men. Praise and/or blame, pat phrases of motivation, are measured out with no attempt to portray a man.

Biography can of course portray a group without photographing a type, and though we cannot have sketches of all members of the Estates General of 1789, short biographies around a common theme supply unique insights. For instance some historians have brushed away many cobwebs in Roman history by studying the influential alliances of powerful families. Others have done the same for English history. When Tory Sir Robert Peel in 1835 damned the Whigs for being "all cousins" he was assessing a political situation found over and over again. Individuals combine, families unite. Families fell as did rulers, but families had heirs. Cousinship and marriage guaranteed continuity and stability. Nevertheless one must not claim too much simply because people had relatives. The formula is not the thing, and we are only suggesting that biographers and their readers consider closely knit groups as well as individuals.

The History of Biography

Biography in evolution illumines the history of ideas, for to create it as opposed to "typography" took centuries. Egyptian inscriptions were self-glorification, Babylonian chronicles egotistical eulogies. The Greeks advanced slightly, but though biography took definite literary form among them, they were slow to conceive an evolving individual and so produced little but encomia, fragmentary and "typical." *Exempla* were all their goal. Yet by the fourth century B. C. men were replacing types. Whereas Thucydides used biography only to illuminate the course of history, Plato avowed his debt to men and not the trees or the country. Five centuries later Plutarch used the specific to prove the general. Others told "all," and so enable later biographers to create a flesh and blood Caesar and Cicero. In the middle ages saints and rulers got most attention but were generally portrayed as ideal, even stock figures. Didactic, edifying, stylized, saints' lives seemed scarcely more than a collection of deeds and borrowed anecdotes. At the same time because of their central purpose, the authors excluded irrelevant detail and some at least set forth the living man. Edification alone never bequeathed such gems as Einhard's Charlemagne and Joinville's Louis IX.

The description of man, inwardly and outwardly, that Burckhardt credited to Renaissance Italians did not immediately supersede "typography," but in time the recovery of ancient models, patriotism, and Protestantism breathed life into stock figures. Historians resurrected men who had long slept in dust and oblivion; they studied causation through the aims of individuals. They wrote as poets to delight and instruct; they also wrote as scholars, joining unpublished materials with their own experience. Because biography set forth the true and inward business of affairs, it had great profit; because it must instruct, the authors by no means indulged in unqualified eulogy. The day was far off when Carlyle could write, "How delicate, how decent is English biography, bless its mealy mouth."

As society changed and uniformity gave way to diversity, biography became more popular and varied. The bars were down. Vico, the Italian philosopher, saw biographical sketches as the way to trace the progress of the human mind; the novelists cast their fiction in biographical form; the *philosophes* made individuals the mouthpieces of their ideas. As man became more and more the measure of all things, the biographer became an analyst, a psychologist. To push the growing maturity came autobiography whose value, attested by Goethe, was exemplified by Rousseau, though, by contrast, the *Memoirs* of the historian Gibbon are those of a man who could never descend from his dignity. Whatever the impulse to write "confessions," the effect was to make biography more revealing. As it became more mature, men saw it as the species of history best adapted to teach wisdom. The biographer went behind the scenes whereas the historian was concerned with the actors on stage. New subjects entered the scene with the emergence of the first industrial society and the consequent leveling of social ranks—the merchant and the adventurer.

Not only were these changes taking place but contemporaries were aware of them. Men saw the limitations of biography and difficulty of composition yet lauded the value and recognized the appeal. They prescribed that the biographer should gather materials diligently but always selectively and write with judgment and understanding. He should choose an important subject, avoid invention, and seek to penetrate the man behind the mask. He should not mistake chance for design, bend facts to a theory, or seek popular applause. Simplicity not embellishment should mark the style, and the writer should seek a happy mixture of "times" and "life." Biography like a lantern lighted the steps of the traveler; it was no medium for "industrious judges and laborious drones." Now that divine right no longer held sway, princes had given way to merchants and even criminals, but whatever the subject biography struck observers as the proper history for young people: it was vicarious experience. No wonder then that the eighteenth century bore a huge crop of biographies, of which an important phase was the extensive biographical dictionary.

Throughout the nineteenth century the exploits of divers individuals and the steady rise of the social sciences alike furthered the conviction that since man was the measure of all things, he was the proper study of mankind. Biography had arrived and what came after was scarcely more than a variation on an established theme. Freudian concepts, it is true, prompted psychographs but the words were newer than the practice. The rise of minorities and new states introduced new heroes but not new techniques. Since the later nineteenth century the biographical dictionary, national or topical, and the growing tendency to reinterpret the past in terms of closely-knit groups have expanded the art. Biography does not stand still. Not only do new subjects find their author but old ones are re-examined.

However ancient the art of biography, it is by no means uniformly penetrating. Biographies are still written, as Charles Dickens put it, "by somebody who lived next door to the people, rather than inside 'em." The stereotype—the progressive, the communist, the dictator—is still with us, though a greater affliction is the author who knows precisely what his hero thought at 3 A.M. January 31, 1869, and documents his knowledge quite meticulously. Such procedure may deceive readers woefully. On the other hand an unrestrained devotion to bald fact may deceive them just as much. When John Aubrey, the seventeenth-century English biographer, decided to write a life he jotted down everything he could remember about the man—friends, sayings, appearance, actions, and reading. Later on he added, revised, and arranged. Some biographers have stopped with the first part of Aubrey's practice and by concentrating on particulars have missed the whole. Nevertheless such intense pursuit of fact has provided substantial footing for imaginative historians.

Makers of the European World since 1500

To plunge into the historical process is to tear a seamless web, yet the historian must make that plunge. He will regard himself as fortunate if he can seize on a period when he can justify a new start. Such a period occurred about 1500. In order to discover how biography illustrates the centuries since, the following pages will correlate men of action and men of ideas. Among the first will be rulers, soldiers, explorers, and merchants; among the second, philosophers, scientists, and artists. Space does not permit citing a sizable proportion of influential men, or consideration of those cited, but teachers and students should apply the suggestions scattered throughout to other men and other activities.

The Renaissance and Reformation, the Scientific Revolution, the National State, and the Expansion of Europe, all intersecting, comprise the seedbed from which subsequent history has sprung. Through these forces men discovered themselves, the brave new world about them, and the vast universe of which their world was part. They discovered new customs and beliefs; they invigorated their literature and art; they found new outlets in trade and industry, new ways of living together, and, alas, new areas of friction. Who were they and how did they influence the history of Europe and indeed of the larger world since 1500? In answering this question we must not separate men of deeds from men of ideas or differentiate between politics, religion, business, science, and arts. Throughout history many men have bestridden different activities, and developments in one sphere have impinged upon those in others. No ruler, merchant, or scientist lived wholly unto himself; no enterprise was independent of others. Nevertheless, it is convenient to stress one theme at a time.

Let us begin with politics, the aspect of development which more than any other drew upon the total resources of mankind. By the sixteenth century the territorial state was emerging. Its rulers exercised absolute power in finance, war, trade, and religion and in the process enhanced their political power. They reduced the nobility, the church, and the cities, whatever indeed stood in their path. At the same time they found allies—businessmen who profited from orderly government and publicists who preferred royal policies to earlier anarchy. To be sure universal empire continued in the face of centrifugal forces, but sooner or later every territorial state was headed by a ruler who illustrated and directed nationalistic forces. Henry VIII and Elizabeth I of England, Henry IV and Louis XIV in France, Ferdinand and Philip II in Spain, the Great Elector and Frederick the Great in Prussia, Gustavus Adolphus in Sweden, Maria Theresa and Joseph II in Austria, Ivan, Peter, and Catherine in Russia are only the more spectacular examples of a type that appeared even in small states. Indeed several of the rulers specified helped by their abilities and ambitions to transform small states into powerful ones. Even when policies differed, objectives were identical.

The merchants, about whom we know far less than rulers, favored governmental regulation of production, trade, and consumption. They secured laws excluding or penalizing foreign competitors and subsidizing their own exchange of domestic products for necessities that could be consumed and luxuries that could be traded. Such economic nationalism, inextricably tied to political nationalism, was also bound up with overseas expansion, commercial and colonial. Men sailed the seas for various reasons—curiosity, religion, glory, profit—but their backers, whether kings or capitalists, had one objective, profits, profits in power or money. Rulers sought trained seamen and a strong navy; merchants sought materials, markets, and investments.

Desire for profits, territory, seamen, materials would in itself have accomplished little, had not physical science, mathematics, and medicine made exploration possible. During the twelfth and thirteenth centuries, it is true, travelers—the most famous being Marco Polo—had penetrated remote parts of the world, but they were landsmen. In the fifteenth century Prince Henry the Navigator of Portugal sought a sea route to the Indies. Aided by cartographers and astronomers, he sent expeditions down the African coast, and, though he never realized his dream, a generation after his death Vasco da Gama rounded Africa to give Portugal, however briefly, the lead in exploration. Contemporaneously Columbus, no less inspired, discovered America. Thirty years later Magellan circumnavigated the earth, and henceforth the oceans became the highway of expansion. Then exploration required improvements in navigation, shipbuilding, and medicine, and the greatest names in science—Copernicus, Galileo, and Kepler, Paracelsus, Vesalius, and Harvey, Gilbert, Descartes, and Newton—directly or indirectly aided the expansion process. Given practical impulses and necessary knowledge, all sorts and conditions of men set in motion a chain of events transforming every area of thought and action.

While political and economic nationalism was eroding universal empire, and expansion was exporting European rivalries, as well as goods and ideas, to Asia, Africa, and the Americas, another powerful expression of national patriotism was occurring in religion, which rulers found as useful as trade to their aspirations. The repudiation of papal authority, though not limited to countries that became Protestant, was most obvious there. Here the most influential figure was Martin Luther. As Luther moved further and further from the Roman Church, he appealed more and more to reformers. His ringing response to condemnation as a heretic, "I cannot do otherwise. Here I stand," proclaimed the Protestant temper. In support of his stand he appealed to the German nobility, condemned Catholic abuses, reformed the liturgy, and translated the Bible into German. Though he broke with the witty, critical Erasmus—reformer rather than revolutionary—he found in Melanchthon a scholarly link with the learned. Soon his ideas penetrated outside Germany, sometimes to triumph as in Scandanavia, sometimes to influence the native reform movement as in England, sometimes to fail of lasting impression.

Whatever the import of Luther as a symbol of the Protestant Revolt, neither his personality nor ideas should obscure the impact of other reformers. The Swiss Zwingli, also moved by political considerations, went further than Luther in stripping off ceremonial. French John Calvin, more intellectual than Luther or Zwingli, would have made Geneva into a City of God where churchmen would direct and laymen execute the administration of political, moral, and economic activities. In England no reformer dominated the scene though Thomas Cranmer left an imperishable monument in the Book of Common Prayer. Many other men in several countries propagated reform ideas, often differing extensively from one another. Some stressed theology, some politics, others social reform; some appealed to the upper classes, others to the lower. Under such circumstances accusations of heresy flew back and forth and on occasion led to persecution. The most famous victim of Protestant persecution was Michael Servetus, Spanish-born scientist and anti-trinitarian, burned at Geneva. We must remember also Thomas More and Cranmer, the first a victim of Henry VIII, the second of Queen Mary.

Although religion joined politics and economics to nourish the national state, the earlier ideal of one world still found active support, in political and religious circles alike. The papacy continuously sought the unity of Christendom. Perhaps its most potent instrument was the Society of Jesus, organized in 1540 by a crusading Spanish soldier, Ignatius Loyola. Soon and better known as the Jesuits, the society worked unremittingly by education, missions, and political influence to counteract Protestantism. On the political side Emperor Charles V was striving to maintain, and even expand, the Holy Roman Empire. He ruled Burgundy, Spain, the Netherlands, Naples, Sicily, Sardinia, Milan, Austria, and Germany. No less industrious and masterful than the national kings, he sought to hold his sprawling territories together through the force of his personality. Dynasticism was his ruling emotion, and to maintain power he, who wanted peace, was constantly at war.

War was the measure of his failure, for to restore the unity of Roman Christendom was impossible: centrifugal forces proved too powerful. The rise of vernacular literature accompanied other national impulses. Men worshipped and sang in their own tongue. They wrote the histories of their own country in that tongue, and these along with poetry and drama, even religion and science, in the vernacular strengthened patriotism. Often, to be sure, patriotism was less devotion to one's own country than hostility to others, but nonetheless it shaped national and international policy alike.

The national state had other advocates besides those specified, and among them none was more useful than the political philosopher. Each— the Italian Machiavelli, the French Bodin, and the English Hooker, for instance—differed from the other but all testified to the spread of nationalism. Among these men Machiavelli has excited the greatest attention; all too often considered the very incarnation of amoral politics, he was a devoted patriot and an advocate of law and the public good.

Throughout the centuries since 1500 the forces that gave birth to the modern world influenced its development. In every country, in every generation men distinguished in politics, religion, economics, and the arts and sciences extended the activities already sketched. Nowhere did the manifold features of the modern state appear more clearly than in England. The great Tudor monarchs, Henry VII, Henry VIII, and Elizabeth, with their ministers, Cardinal Wolsey and Lord Burghley, strengthened the central government, ran it efficiently, and utilized every resource they could. The break with Rome was state made for state ends, and the dominant figure was a ruthless dynast intent on a male heir and greedy for power. In promoting his aims Henry VIII capitalized on ancient hostility to the papacy and marshalled a mixed array of supporters—merchants, reformers, and intellectuals—to bolster his secular authority by ecclesiastical pre-eminence. His daughter Elizabeth consolidated his achievement at home and extended English power abroad with the help of merchants like Thomas Gresham and seamen like John Hawkins, Francis Drake, and Walter Raleigh. Coinciding with practical accomplishment were the glories of literature and thought as summed up in Shakespeare and Richard Hakluyt, Hooker and Gilbert.

If political leadership declined in the seventeenth century, economic, intellectual, and artistic achievement did not. To appreciate the "age of genius" one only need examine the legacies of Francis Bacon, Harvey, Robert Boyle, and Newton in science, Thomas Hobbes, James Harrington, and John Locke in political philosophy, William Petty and Christopher Wren in half a dozen fields, Lionel Cranfield and Josiah Child in business and politics, John Donne, John Milton, and John Dryden in literature. In so doing, however, one must remember, as always, that back of these brightest stars were many who would ornament any age. In the realm of politics, furthermore, one must consider the Earl of Strafford, the minister of Charles I, Oliver Cromwell, in whose brief tenure so much of modern England had its start, and the Earl of Shaftesbury who had wit enough to choose John Locke as his secretary. Time and again, be it said, the activities of men in one area intersected with those of men in another, and indeed the same man often left his mark in several spheres.

Across the Channel, France had equal intellectual prestige and, during the seventeenth century, far greater political influence. Throughout much of the preceding century her rulers had served her badly as they frittered away her resources in wars, civil and foreign alike. Religion largely caused the civil strife, manifested in such frightful excesses as St. Bartholomew's massacre, but in 1589 with the accession of Henry IV, a Protestant turned Catholic—Paris is worth a mass—the tension eased. He pacified religious extremists and strengthened the central government by reducing taxes, encouraging agriculture and industry, improving transportation, and cutting administrative costs. In these respects he reflected the contemporary trend towards centralized monarchy and also anticipated the enlightened despots of the eighteenth century. His real successor was not a crowned head but Cardinal Richelieu who continued to strengthen the central government, support trade, and maintain order. Once these men had laid the foundation of strong government, their successors maintained the same policies.

Although France reached her political peak under Louis XIV, his regime planted the seeds of decline. He governed absolutely in the conviction of his divine right. He conquered territories, patronized the arts, put recalcitrant nobles to work, and centralized the government still further; in all these actions he became a very model of a modern despot. To carry out his policies he appointed able men and rewarded them well. Such a man was Colbert, controller-general of finances, whose responsibility extended to trade, industry, and colonization. Unhappily his peaceful achievements were cancelled by Louis' ambition to dominate Europe and to force conformity in France. To this latter end Louis so persecuted the Huguenots that several hundred thousand of them left France to live among his enemies, taking with them their funds and their skills. As foreign opposition mounted, glory gave way to bankruptcy. The roots of the French Revolution ran far back of 1789. Fortunately the history of France has other marks of distinction than those of politics and power: Montaigne and Molière in literature, Descartes and Pascal in science and philosophy alike, are a truer measure of her greatness.

Spain's golden age spanned the sixteenth century, following the rise of Ferdinand and Isabella and largely terminating with Philip II, though for another half century the cracks in the imperial structure were scarcely visible. During the years of greatness monarchs controlled a turbulent nobility, exploited the *forms* of representative government, improved justice and administration, reduced the Moors and Jews, and governed a huge overseas empire, to make Spain the first power in Europe. Yet trade and industry gained little attention and less respect. Overseas enterprise was over-extended; colonial rivalries meant war, and war meant debt;

bureaucracy strangled efficiency. Philip II, able and industrious, was so conscientious that he never did one day what he could postpone to the next lest he fail to weigh all the possibilities. Meanwhile, England, France, and Holland eroded Spanish power. Setbacks turned into defeats, defeats into demoralization, demoralization into corruption. By the mid-seventeenth century Spain had become a pawn where once she had been the queen. Decline, however, should not obscure the legacy that went far beyond empire: Cervantes, Velasquez and El Greco, and the dramatists bequeathed far more to posterity than the treasure fleet.

To describe Spain is to recall the Netherlands, divided in language and religion as in political evolution. Although the southern provinces, now Belgium, remained in Spanish hands until 1713, when they passed to Austria, the northern provinces, ultimately known as Holland, moved towards unity under William the Silent in the late sixteenth century as hostility to Spain and economic interests triumphed over religious differences. Bankers and merchants no less than rulers built up a strong state and overseas empire, one graced also by such immortals as Rembrandt and Grotius. In Sweden Gustavus Adolphus increased his country's prestige abroad and improved administration at home. Russia too evolved in a fashion often parallel to that of western European nations. In the mid-sixteenth century before he went to the extremes that won him notoriety as "the Terrible," Czar Ivan strengthened the central government at the expense of the nobles, but their strength and the absence of a class committed to strong monarchy prevented fulfillment of his policy. Not until the coming of Peter the Great did Russia match the West.

If Germany and Italy, the scenes of anarchy and war, remained geographical expressions until the nineteenth century, they were the scenes of many changes in trade, finance, and industry, as well as unsurpassed achievements in art, science, and literature. In Florence the Medici family gained enormous power through its banking interests and for a time not only ruled the city but controlled the papacy. Dictators also controlled several other cities. Happily the history of Italy did not evolve wholly in terms of dictators or even merchants and bankers. Leonardo da Vinci, Michelangelo, Galileo, and a host of others made Italy a magnet for centuries. In Germany the Fuggers are only the best known in a veritable hive of merchants. Their enterprises penetrated throughout Europe, and so great was their power, so diverse were their contacts, that they exercised far more authority than the nominal heads of states. As elsewhere philosophers and scientists were leaving their mark and the names of Kepler and Leibnitz but suggest the rich quality of German culture.

During the Enlightenment men continued as important as ever although the order of importance changed. If the kings departed or at least fell back—in several countries—the captains did not, nor did merchants, artists, philosophers, or scientists. In Prussia, Austria, and Russia, where kings ruled as well as reigned, the "enlightened despot" was his sixteenth-century predecessor writ large and self conscious. In countries where kings reigned rather than ruled, ministers played the role of bygone Richelieus and Burghleys. Merchants, industrialists, and entrepreneurs extended their influence. Men of ideas had broad interests as before and, though seldom in public office, had intimate contacts with men in power.

In the largest sense the Enlightenment derived its character from those men of ideas who in time created the revolutionary era which came after. Though no country failed to swell the cultural sum, space permits only a sampling. France, its political priority gone, had no superior in intellectual leadership, much of it in political thought. Montesquieu in law and politics, Rousseau in politics and education, Voltaire in literature, politics, and history, Bayle and Diderot as critics and encyclopaedists, had followers all across Europe and in the Americas. More limited in their direct appeal but very distinguished were Buffon the naturalist, Lavoisier the chemist, and Turgot who combined economics, philosophy, and politics both in their practical and theoretical aspects. Great Britain, less spectacularly but still substantially represented, offered David Hume, historian and philosopher, Edward Gibbon, historian, Samuel Johnson, biographer and lexicographer, Edmund Burke, political theorist as well as public servant, and Jeremy Bentham, law reformer—men whose impact is still everywhere about us. Moreover, though John Wesley does not fit the pattern of the Enlightenment, he warrants attention for his share in revitalizing religion; the same applies to William Wilberforce, the anti-slavery leader.

Germany also had many entries in the calendar of great men. The universal Goethe still stands as the greatest name in German literature, while the pre-eminence of Kant in philosophy and Bach in music is not less marked. Nor dare one omit Mozart in music, Herder in history and anthropology, and Schiller in literature. The lack of a German nation only made German intellectual achievement more universal in its appeal. In Sweden Linnaeus indulged the contemporary enthusiasm for scientific classification and, by appreciating the close relation between organisms and their environment, was a forerunner of Charles Darwin. The Italian philosopher Vico who deepened and broadened the study of history has but recently won the attention he deserved; his fellow-countryman Beccaria outshone all but a very few as a law reformer. Behind these men and their unnamed fellows were dozens more modest in attainment but no less reflective of current ideas.

· When we turn to individual countries we shall see how men of action to some degree translated ideas into policy. In Great Britain royal absolutism yielded to oligarchy. Robert Walpole largely created the office of prime minister and the concept of cabinet unity; often portrayed as a corruptionist, he must be remembered as a conscientious and able leader who for two decades governed his country. When in time his policy of peace and economy no longer satisfied influential people, the aggressive, brilliant William Pitt provided the leadership necessary to defeat France in the great war for empire. A generation later, a second William Pitt led the country in the titanic struggle with revolutionary France. Important as were these ministers of state, as well as generals like Marlborough, Wolfe, Clive, and Wellington and admirals like Nelson, England owed prestige no less to James Watt and Richard Arkwright in industry, Jethro Tull and Arthur Young in agriculture, James Cook in empire building, and the artists and scientists already mentioned.

The contemporary eclipse of the French monarchy owing to royal ineptitude, bankruptcy, military defeat, and territorial losses paved the way to revolution. Neither good intentions nor piecemeal reforms provided any barrier against such extremists as Robespierre and the terror they inspired. In time this phase passed and gave the military dictator his chance. Napoleon, however, quickly demonstrated genius in law and administration as well as on the battlefield. Neither France nor Europe would be the same again. The ideas of Voltaire and Rousseau, the overthrow of the monarchy, and the conquests of Napoleon, which spread the revolutionary doctrines throughout Europe, guaranteed a new age.

Prussia, Austria, and Russia during much of the eighteenth century were better served by their kings than France, though no better than several smaller states whose rulers were prompted by the same ambition and circumstances. Prussia, of all the European states, had the most spectacular rise, owing chiefly to the ability and devotion of its rulers. From dismal beginnings in 1640 the electorate of Brandenburg-Prussia evolved into the powerful kingdom of Prussia. The transformation was above all the achievement of three men—the Great Elector, Frederick William I, and Frederick the Great. All sought efficiency and economy, all made the country a force in European politics. The first and third added much territory, and Frederick the Great sought to match his military and administrative success with cultural distinction.

In Austria Maria Theresa, aware of what was happening in Prussia, introduced similar administrative, financial, and commercial reforms with beneficial results. Her son and successor, Joseph II, perhaps the most self-conscious of all "enlightened despots," sought to improve the lot of the serfs, but the resentment aroused by his changes frustrated his plans and prompted him to describe himself as one who with the best of intentions had succeeded in nothing but making enemies. Russia during the century had two remarkable rulers. Peter, fascinated by the technical achievement of Western Europe, modernized administration, developed industry, improved education, and reduced the nobility and the church. In the realm of policy his successor was Catherine the Great, who extended the boundaries and put Russia more firmly into the European world.

Some years before her death the ideals and tactics of the French revolutionaries made a mockery of what often seems the fun and games of the enlightened despots: Robespierre and his associates were playing for keeps. Nevertheless, neither abstract ideals nor concrete reforms could alone defend France against the hatred generated by the fear that no more than the natural air would the winds of revolutionary doctrine remain within her borders. The French response to the foreign crusade was Napoleon. Though ultimately defeated, he was less the victim of the rulers who led the crusade than of the force he had unleashed to score his own triumphs—national patriotism—especially as it came to the surface in Spain, Germany, and Russia. For the time being, however, the dynasts led by Metternich, the Austrian foreign minister, kept this force in chains.

Nationalism was not the only leaf which France's enemies took from her book. The rulers of Prussia and Russia at least inaugurated reforms. In Prussia Baron Stein led the way to the abolition of serfdom and to military, political, and educational reforms, though many were soon watered down. The same was true in Russia where Alexander I, with the counsel of Michael Speransky, administrator and theorist, seemed likely to extend the schemes of the enlightened despots with fundamental social and political reforms, but he never fulfilled the promise of his gestures.

During the nineteenth and twentieth centuries new men, if not new forces, were shaping the scene. Monarchs, with few exceptions, played small parts; the same was true of soldiers, sailors, and ecclesiastics. On the other hand ministers of state bulked large; explorers by land rather than by sea rivalled Columbus and Magellan; empire-builders came thick; industrialists, merchants, and bankers made rulers their clients and the nation's business their own. In the realm of ideas men more and more confined their attention to one province, but more provinces were cultivated intensively. Yet these changes represented no total break. Every sort of man who has played a large role in the last 150 years had his forerunners in the preceding three hundred, but the closer we get to our own day the number competing for attention increases. As earlier the activities of all men have continued to intersect on every hand. Similarly the history of all nations has had much in common, though each has had its peculiar heroes as well as those who could have appeared in any country.

In Queen Victoria Great Britain had one of the few monarchs who won more than casual notice. At her accession English royalty had sunk to its lowest level, but as ruler and woman she restored its prestige. As queen she was well served by her ministers, the most famous being Peel, Palmerston, Disraeli, and Gladstone, who helped to make the nineteenth century Britain's century. Political democracy and social reforms, economic growth and imperialism alike built that prestige. Throughout private citizens had a large part—in social reform Robert Owen and William Cobbett, Florence Nightingale and the Fabian socialists, the house of Rothschild in business, Gibbon Wakefield, Cecil Rhodes, David Livingstone, and Frederick Lugard in empire building, just to name a few. The arts and sciences had equal quality and quantity as the names of John Stuart Mill in several realms, Newman in religion, Darwin in science, Macaulay in history, Dickens in the novel testify.

France had no ruler to match Victoria, but Napoleon III, anxious to recapture the glories of the great Napoleon, instituted economic and social policies that gave the country a prestige far more lasting than political power. Only a small fraction of the men who made France a cultural mecca can be named. In social thought St. Simon, Louis Blanc, and Pierre Proudhon, in political thought Tocqueville and Georges Sorel, in science the physiologist Claude Bernard and Louis Pasteur, in literature Stendhal, Balzac, and Hugo, and in art Daumier, Renoir, and Cezanne will be remembered as long as men are interested in human achievement. Far more than the paltry heroes of the moment they summed up the highest aspirations of Frenchmen and indeed of all mankind. Not all to be sure was glorious, for as elsewhere the shoddy opportunist flourished, and no better instance can be cited of the seamy side than the Dreyfus case, at once a national disgrace and a national purge.

What has been said of France may also be said of Prussia and in the broader sense of Germany. No ruler need concern us, but one minister must, namely, Bismarck, the architect of the German Empire, 1870–1918. His remarkable success in diplomacy, and to a much less degree in other areas, made that empire the most powerful state on the continent. Nevertheless, his achievement, however impressive, no more summed up the essential legacy of Germany to posterity than had that of Frederick the Great a century before. Musicians such as Beethoven and Wagner, a host of scientists such as Paul Ehrlich, Alexander Humboldt, and Roentgen, historians such as Ranke, philosophers such as Hegel and Nietzsche, and Karl Marx bequeathed more lasting legacies.

In Italy we look chiefly to the architects of Italian unification, Mazzini the dreamer, Garibaldi the warrior, and Cavour the statesman, each one essential, each one interwoven with the other. In Russia two monarchs reflected basic changes in outlook, Nicholas I the autocrat and Alexander II the reformer, but as elsewhere the men of deeds must give way to the men of ideas, to Leo Tolstoy, novelist, philosopher, and social reformer, Dostoyevsky the novelist, Tschaikowsky the musician, Kropotkin and Bakunin the social philosophers. In the Habsburg empire men of ideas held their own with those in other countries, but political leadership was totally lacking: the futility of Emperor Francis Joseph was his realm's dissolution. That the larger countries did not monopolize distinction is clear, though in lesser countries the smaller stage gave greater opportunity to men of ideas than men of deeds. No dramatist in the nineteenth century overshadowed Henrik Ibsen of Norway, and the rise of Existentialist philosophy in the twentieth century has given immortality to Soren Kierkegaard of Denmark.

As we close in on our own day, the difficulty of singling out the men likely to influence the future increases. Every morning's newspaper has a new hero. Time and circumstance have not yet worn away the accidental hero who will not survive the next decade or reduced him who is in everyone's mouth today to next week's forgotten man. Tradition lies heavy upon us and we look oftener to the political leader than to the obscure men who shape his decisions and all our destinies. Perhaps this outcome is inevitable, for the very power of some men depends on their obscurity which in some instances they actually seek. Yet the cult of the mystery man must not be overdone; after all the man out front is the public idol. There have always been "grey eminences," lost to history's pages, but by and large the makers of history have been such because they were known to be. The philosophers, artists of every sort—actors, poets, painters, sculptors—historians, scientists, in short the men who have made history, have never needed hidden manipulators.

Among the men of action in the twentieth century Lloyd-George, in peace and war alike, and Churchill, Hitler and Mussolini, Lenin and Trotsky, Stalin and Khrushchev, and Kemal are strong candidates for immortality, in some cases for the worst of reasons. Businessmen still await their biographies (I rule out mere rhapsodies), and they will be better known a generation hence. Men of ideas have already been more adequately memorialized though some already the subjects of biographies may not stand the erosion of time. Among those creators likely to be long remembered are Lord Keynes, economist, Benedetto Croce and Vilfredo Pareto, Italian philosopher and sociologist respectively, Einstein and Rutherford, Thomas Mann and Sigmund Freud, but to cite them is only to underscore gaping omissions, including many men who a hundred years hence may occupy a larger niche than those who now get attention. Nevertheless, today's hero *is* important for today if not for next year.

Whether men are heroes for a day or forever does not always matter. What does matter is that in times of crisis or decision, the human personality is first, that, as Herman Melville put it, "genius, all over the world, stands hand in hand, and one shock of recognition runs the whole circle round." If we cannot in every instance accept Hamlet's eulogy— "What a piece of work is a man! how noble in reason! how infinite in faculty! in form, in moving, how express and admirable! in action how like an angel! in apprehension how like a god! the beauty of the world! the paragon of animals!"—we must not accept his dismissal—"what is this quintessence of dust? Man delights not me." No more than quintessences of dust are men merely political or social or economic animals: they think, they feel, they even play dirty tricks but they also give their lives to causes greater than themselves. They make history, they have the right with Arthur O'Shaughnessy to sing,

We are the music-makers,
And we are the dreamers of dreams,
Wandering by lone sea-breakers,
And sitting by desolate streams;
World-losers and world-forsakers,
On whom the pale moon gleams:
Yet we are the movers and shakers
Of the world for ever, it seems.
With wonderful deathless ditties
We build up the world's great cities,
And out of a fabulous story
We fashion an empire's glory:
One man with a dream, at pleasure,
Shall go forth and conquer a crown;
And three with a new song's measure
Can trample an empire down.

BIBLIOGRAPHY

In the following list I have generally cited the subjects in order of mention. Throughout I have starred the paperbacks.

Nature and History

*Clifford, James L., *Biography as an Art* (N. Y.: Oxford University Press, 1962, 256 pp., $1.75) excellent bibliography.

Garraty, John, *The Nature of Biography* (N. Y.: Knopf, 1957, 289 pp.).

*Hook, Sidney, *The Hero in History* (Boston: Beacon Press, $1.25).

Sixteenth and Seventeenth Centuries (with a few exceptions)

Henry the Eighth. By Francis Hackett (N. Y.: Bantam, 50 cents).

Henry VIII. By A. F. Pollard (N. Y.: Longmans, 1951, 385 pp.).

Queen Elizabeth I. By J. E. Neale (N. Y.: Anchor, $1.45).

The Great Tudors. By Katharine Garvin (London: Eyre and Spottiswoode, 1956, 296 pp.).

The Tudors: personalities and practical politics in sixteenth century England. By Conyers Read (N. Y.: Henry Holt, 1936, 264 pp.).

Henry of Navarre (Henry IV). By H. D. Sedgwick (Indianapolis: Bobbs-Merrill, 1930, 324 pp.).

Louis XIV. By David Ogg (N. Y.: Oxford, 1951, 255 pp.).

The Great Elector. By Ferdinand Schevill (Chicago: University of Chicago Press, 1947, 442 pp.).

Frederick the Great: the ruler, the writer, the man. By G. P. Gooch (N. Y.: Longmans, 1947, 363 pp.).

Gustavus Adolphus. By Michael Roberts (N. Y.: Longmans, 2 vols. 1953, 1958, 528, 564 pp.).

Maria Theresa and Other Studies. By G. P. Gooch (N. Y.: Longmans, 1951, 432 pp.).

The Revolutionary Emperor, Joseph the Second, 1741–1790. By S. K. Padover (N. Y.: Ballou, 1934, 414 pp.).

Ivan the Terrible. By Hans von Eckhardt (N. Y.: Knopf, 1949, 421 pp.).

*Peter the Great. By Vasili Klyuchevsky (N. Y.: Vintage, $1.25).

Peter the Great and the Emergence of Russia. By B. H. Sumner (London: English Universities Press, 1950, 216 pp.).

Catherine the Great, Autocrat and Empress of all Russia. By Ian Grey (N. Y.: Lippincott, 1961, 254 pp.).

*Marco Polo. By Maurice Collis (N. Y.: New Directions, $1.35).

Henry the Navigator. By Elaine Sanceau (London, N. Y.: Hutchinson & Co., 1946, 144 pp.).

Vasco da Gama and his Successors, 1460–1580. By K. G. Jayne (London: Methuen, 1910, 325 pp.).

*Christopher Columbus, Mariner. By S. E. Morison (N. Y.: Mentor, 50 cents).

Conqueror of the Seas: Life of Magellan. By Stefan Zweig (N. Y.: Viking Press, 1938, 335 pp.).

*The World of Copernicus (Sun Stand Thou Still). By Angus Armitage (N. Y.: Mentor, 50 cents).

*From Copernicus to Einstein. By Hans Reichenbach (N. Y.: Wisdom Library, 95 cents).

*Crime of Galileo. By Giorgio de Santillana (Chicago: University of Chicago Press, $1.75).

*Men of Mathematics. By E. T. Bell (N. Y.: Random House, $2.25).

*The Watershed: a biography of Johannes Kepler. By Arthur Koestler (N. Y.: Anchor, 95 cents).

*The Great Doctors. By Henry Sigerist (N. Y.: Anchor, $1.25).

*Men of Medicine. By Katherine Shippen (N. Y.: Viking, $1.25).

Paracelsus. By Henry M. Pachter (N. Y.: Schuman, 1951, 360 pp.).

William Harvey: his life and times, his discoveries, his methods. By Louis Chauvois (London: Hutchinson, 1957, 271 pp.).

Diderot and Descartes. By Aram Vartanian (Princeton: Princeton University Press, 1953, 336 pp.).

*Sir Isaac Newton. By E. N. Andrade (N. Y.: Anchor, 95 cents).

*Here I Stand: a life of Martin Luther. By Roland Bainton (N. Y.: Mentor, 75 cents; N. Y.: Apex, $1.75).

*Erasmus and the Age of the Reformation. By Johan Huizinga (N. Y.: Harper, $1.50).

Melanchthon: the quiet reformer. By C. L. Manschreck (N. Y.: Abingdon Press, 1958, 350 pp.).

Zwingli, the Reformer: his life and work. By Oskar Farner (N. Y.: Philosophical Library, 1952, 135 pp.).

*John Calvin. By Albert-Marie Schmidt (N. Y.: Harper, $1.50).

Cranmer and the English Reformation. By F. E. Hutchinson (N. Y.: Macmillan, 1951, 188 pp.).

*Christian Scholar in the Age of the Reformation. By E. Harris Harbison (N. Y.: Scribner's, $1.25).

*Spiritual Reformers in the 16th and 17th Centuries. By Rufus Jones (Boston: Beacon, $1.95).

Hunted Heretic: the life and death of Michael Servetus. By Roland Bainton (Boston: Beacon, $1.75).

Thomas More. By R. W. Chambers (Ann Arbor, $1.95).

St. Ignatius of Loyola. By Fr. P. Dudon (Milwaukee: Bruce, 1949, 484 pp.).

The Emperor Charles V: the growth and destiny of a man and a world-empire. By Karl Brandi (N. Y.: Knopf, 1939, 655 pp.).

Machiavelli and Renaissance Italy. By J. R. Hale (N. Y.: Macmillan, 1960, 244 pp.).

Henry VII. By Gladys Temperley (Boston: Houghton Mifflin, 1914, 453 pp.).

Wolsey. A. F. Pollard (N. Y.: Longmans, 1929, 393 pp.).

Mr. Secretary Cecil and Queen Elizabeth. By Conyers Read (N. Y.: Knopf, 1955, 510 pp.).

Lord Burghley and Queen Elizabeth. By Conyers Read. (London: Cape, 1960, 603 pp.).

Hawkins of Plymouth. By J. A. Williamson (London: Black, 1949, 348 pp.).

Sir Francis Drake. By J. A. Williamson (N. Y.: Collier, 95 cents).

Raleigh and the British Empire. By David Quinn (N. Y.: Macmillan, 1949, 284 pp.).

Builders of Empire. By J. A. Williamson (Oxford: Clarendon Press, 1952, 297 pp.).

Shakespeare of London. By Marchette Chute (N. Y.: Everyman, $1.65).

Shakespeare. By Mark Van Doren (N. Y.: Anchor, 95 cents).

Francis Bacon: philosopher of industrial science. By Benjamin Farrington (N. Y.: Collier, 95 cents).

Robert Boyle and Seventeenth Century Chemistry. By Marie Boas (Cambridge: Cambridge University Press, 1958, 239 pp.).

Hobbes. By Richard Peters (Baltimore: Penguin, 95 cents).

Harrington and his Oceana. By H. F. R. Smith (Cambridge: Cambridge University Press, 1914, 223 pp.).

John Locke: a biography. By Maurice Cranston (N. Y.: Longmans, 1957, 496 pp.).

Sir William Petty: portrait of a genius. By Eric Strauss (Glencoe, Ill.: Free Press, 1954, 260 pp.).

Christopher Wren. By Nikolaus Pevsner (N. Y.: Universe Books, $1.50).

John Donne. By K. W. Gransden (N. Y.: Longmans, 1954, 197 pp.).

John Milton, Englishman. By James Holly Hanford (N. Y.: Crown, $1.45).

John Dryden: a study of his poetry. By Mark Van Doren (Bloomington: Indiana University Press, $1.75).

Thomas Wentworth, First Earl of Strafford, 1593–1641. By C. V. Wedgwood (London: Cape, 1961, 415 pp.).

Greatness of Oliver Cromwell. By Maurice Ashley (N. Y.: Collier, $1.50).

The First Earl of Shaftesbury. By Louise F. Brown (N. Y.: Appleton, Century, 1933, 350 pp.).

Richelieu and the French Monarchy. By C. V. Wedgwood (London: Hodder and Stoughton, 1949, 204 pp.).

Colbert and a Century of French Mercantilism. By C. W. Cole (N. Y.: Columbia University Press, 1939, 2 vols., 589, 620 pp.).

French Pioneers in the West Indies 1624–64. By N. M. Crouse (N. Y.: Columbia University Press, 1940, 294 pp.).

Montaigne's Discovery of Man. By Donald M. Frame (N. Y.: Columbia University Press, 1955, 202 pp.).

Molière: Man seen through the plays. By Ramon Fernandez (N. Y.: Hill and Wang, $1.25).

Pascal: the emergence of genius. By Emile Calliet (N. Y.: Harper, $1.85).

Cervantes. By Aubrey F. G. Bell (N. Y.: Collier, 95 cents).
Velasquez. By Margaretta Salinger (N. Y.: Abrams, Inc., 95 cents).
El Greco. By John F. Mathews (N. Y.: Abrams, Inc., 95 cents).
William the Silent. By C. V. Wedgwood (London: Cape, 1944, 256 pp.).
Rembrandt. By Gladys Schmitt (N. Y.: Dell, 95 cents).
Michelangelo and Rembrandt. By Emil Ludwig (N. Y.: Ace, 50 cents).
Rubens. By Julius Held (N. Y.: Abrams, Inc., 95 cents).
Life and Works of Grotius. By W. S. M. Knight (London: Sweet and Maxwell, 1925, 304 pp.).
Medici. By Ferdinand Schevill (N. Y.: Harper, $1.45).
Lorenzo dei Medici and Renaissance Italy. C. M. Ady (N. Y.: Macmillan, 1952, 176 pp.).
Leonardo da Vinci. By Kenneth Clark (Baltimore: Penguin, $1.45).
Jacob Fugger, the Rich. By Jacob Strieder (N. Y.: Adelphi Co., 1931, 227 pp.).
Leibniz. By H. W. Carr (N. Y.: Dover, $1.35).

The Enlightenment

Montesquieu: a critical biography. By Robert Shackleton (N. Y.: Oxford University Press, 1961, 432 pp.).
The Spirit of Voltaire. By Norman Torrey (N. Y.: Columbia University Press, 1938, 314 pp.).
Jean-Jacques Rousseau: a critical study of his life and writings. By F. C. Green (Cambridge: Cambridge University Press, 1955, 376 pp.).
Bayle the Sceptic. By Howard Robinson (N. Y.: Columbia University Press, 1931, 334 pp.).
Diderot: the testing years, 1713-1759. By Arthur Wilson (N. Y.: Oxford University Press, 1957, 417 pp.).
*Les Philosophes: the Philosophers of the Enlightenment. By Norman Torrey (N. Y.: Putnam's, $1.65).
Forerunners of Darwin, 1745-1839. By Hiram B. Glass (Baltimore: Johns Hopkins University Press, 1959, 471 pp.).
Antoine Lavoisier: scientist, economist, social reformer. By Douglas McKie (N. Y.: Schuman, 1952, 440 pp.).
Hume. By A. H. Basson (Baltimore: Penguin, 95 cents).
Adam Smith and the Scotland of his Day. By C. R. Fay (Cambridge: Cambridge University Press, 1956, 173 pp.).
Edward Gibbon. By Michael Joyce (N. Y.: Longmans, 1953, 176 pp.).
*Life of Johnson. By James Boswell (abr., N. Y.: Dell, 50 cents; N. Y.: Collier, $1.50; complete, N. Y.: Oxford Press, $3.75).
Burke and the Nature of Politics. By Carl Cone (Lexington: University of Kentucky Press, 1957, 415 pp.).
Jeremy Bentham and the Law. By George W. Keeton (London: Stevens, 1948, 266 pp.).
*John Wesley. By Francis McConnell (N. Y.: Abingdon, $1.75).
William Wilberforce and his Times. By Oliver Warner (London: Batsford, 1962, 174 pp.).
Goethe. By Jeanne Ancelet Hustache (N. Y.: Grove Press, $1.35).
Kant. By S. Koerner (Baltimore: Penguin, 95 cents).
J. S. Bach. By Andre Pirro (N. Y.: Crown, $1.25).

Life and Philosophy of Johann Gottfried Herder. By F. McEachran (Oxford: Clarendon Press, 1939, 98 pp.).

Carl Linnaeus. By K. H. Hagberg (London: Cape, 1952, 264 pp.).

Autobiography of Giambattista Vico (Ithaca: Cornell University Press, 1944, 240 pp.).

Voltaire and Beccaria as reformers of criminal law. By Marcello Maestro (N. Y.: Columbia University Press, 1942, 177 pp.).

Three Criminal Law Reformers: Beccaria, Bentham, Romilly. By Coleman Phillipson (N. Y.: Dutton, 1923, 344 pp.).

Sir Robert Walpole: the making of a statesman. By J. H. Plumb (N. Y.: Houghton Mifflin, 1956, 363 pp.).

Chatham. By J. H. Plumb (London: Collins, 1953, 159 pp.).

William Pitt. By John W. Derry (London: Batsford, 1962, 160 pp.).

Marlborough, His Life and Times. By Winston Churchill (N. Y.: Scribner's, 6 vols., 1933–38).

Wolfe at Quebec. By Christopher Hibbert (Cleveland: World Publishing Co., 1961).

Clive of India. By R. J. Minney (London: Jarrolds, 1957, 264 pp.).

The Duke; being an account of the . . . 1st Duke of Wellington. By Richard Aldington. (N. Y.: Viking Press, 1943, 405 pp.).

Nelson the Sailor. By Russell Grenfell (N. Y.: Macmillan, 1950, 235 pp.).

*Kings and Desperate Men. By Louis Kronenberger (N. Y.: Knopf, $1.45).

James Watt and the History of Steam Power. By I. B. Hart (N. Y.: Schuman, 1949, 250 pp.).

An Eighteenth Century Industrialist. Peter Stubs of Warrington, 1756–1806. By T. S. Ashton (Manchester: Manchester University Press, 1961, 156 pp.).

The Strutts and the Arkwrights, 1758–1830. By R. S. Fitton and A. P. Wadsworth (Manchester: Manchester University Press, 1958, 361 pp.).

A London Merchant. By Lucy Sutherland (London: Oxford University Press, 1933, 164 pp.).

Cook and the Opening of the Pacific. By J. A. Williamson (London: Hodder and Stoughton, 1948, 251 pp.).

Robespierre and the French Revolution. By J. M. Thompson (N. Y.: Macmillan, 1953, 180 pp.).

Napoleon Bonaparte: his rise and fall. By J. M. Thompson (N. Y.: Oxford University Press, 1952, 463 pp.).

*The Mind of Napoleon. By J. C. Herold (N. Y.: Columbia University Press, $1.95).

The Potsdam Führer: Frederick William I, Father of Prussian Militarism. By Robert Ergang (N. Y.: Columbia University Press, 1941, 290 pp.).

Nineteenth and Twentieth Centuries

Metternich. By Constantin de Grunwald (London: Falcon Press, 1953, 334 pp.).

Baron Stein, Enemy of Napoleon. By Constantin de Grunwald (London: Cape, 1936, 321 pp.).

Alexander I of Russia: the man who defeated Napoleon. By L. I. Strakhovsky (N. Y.: W. W. Norton, 1947, 302 pp.).

Michael Speransky, Statesman of Imperial Russia. By Marc Raeff (The Hague: M. Nijhoff, 1957, 358 pp.).

Queen Victoria. By Lytton Strachey (N. Y.: Harcourt, 1921, 434 pp.).

Sir Robert Peel. By A. A. Ramsay (N. Y.: Dodd, Mead, 1928, 385 pp.).

Palmerston, 1784–1865. By Philip Guedalla (N. Y.: Putnam's, 1927, 548 pp.).

sraeli: his life and personality. By Hesketh Pearson (N. Y.: Grosset and Dunlap, $1.45).

adstone: a biography. By Philip Magnus (London: Murray, 1954, 482 pp.).

bert Owen. By G. D. H. Cole (London: Benn, 1925, 267 pp.).

he Life of William Cobbett. By G. D. H. Cole (London: Home and Van Thal, 1947, 455 pp.).

Florence Nightingale. By Cecil Woodham-Smith (London: Constable, 1950, 615 pp.).

This Litle Band of Prophets: The British Fabians. By Anne Freemantle (N. Y.: Mentor, 75 cents).

The Rothschilds. By Frederic Morton (London: Athenaeum, 1962, 305 pp.).

The Amazing Career of Edward Gibbon Wakefield. By A. J. Harrop (London: Allen & Unwin, 1928, 253 pp.).

Cecil Rhodes. By S. G. Millin (N. Y.: Harper, 1933, 449 pp.).

The White Nile. By Alan Moorehead (N. Y.: Dell, 75 cents).

Lugard. By Margery Perham (Fair Lawn, N. J.: Essential Books, 1956–60, 2 vols.).

Life of John Stuart Mill. By Michael St. John Packe (N. Y.: Macmillan, 1954, 567 pp.).

The Life of Newman. By Robert Sencourt (London: Dacre Press, 1948, 314 pp.).

Darwin's Century. By Loren Eiseley (N. Y.: Anchor, $1.45).

Lord Macaulay, Victorian Liberal. By Richard C. Beatty (Norman: University of Oklahoma Press, 1938, 387 pp.).

Charles Dickens, a critical introduction. By K. J. Fielding (N. Y. Longmans, 1958, 218 pp.).

Napoleon III: the modern emperor. By Robert Sencourt (London: Benn, 1933, 383 pp.).

The French Faust, Henri de Saint-Simon. By Mathurin M. Dondo (N. Y.: Philosophical Library, 1955, 253 pp.).

Louis Blanc. By Leo A. Loubère (Evanston: Northwestern University Press, 1961, 256 pp.).

Marx, Proudhon, and European Socialism. By John H. Jackson (N. Y.: Macmillan, 1958, 192 pp.).

Alexis De Tocqueville: a biographical study in political science. By J. P. Mayer (N. Y.: Harper, $1.25).

Georges Sorel: prophet without honor. By Richard Humphrey (Cambridge: Harvard University Press, 1951, 246 pp.).

Claude Bernard and his Place in the History of Ideas. Reino Virtanen (Lincoln: University of Nebraska Press, 1960, 156 pp.).

Life of Pasteur. By René Vallery-Radot (N. Y.: Dover, $2.00).

Stendhal: notes on a novelist. By R. M. Adams (N. Y.: Noonday Press, $1.45).

Honoré de Balzac, a biography. By Herbert J. Hunt (London: University of London Press, 1957, 198 pp.).

The Career of Victor Hugo. By E. M. Grant (Cambridge: Harvard University Press, 1945, 365 pp.).

Daumier. By Robert Rey. (N. Y.: Abrams, Inc., 95 cents).

Renoir. By Milton S. Fox (N. Y.: Abrams, Inc., 95 cents).

Cezanne. By Theodore Rousseau (N. Y.: Abrams. Inc., 95 cents).

The Dreyfus Case, a Reassessment. By Guy Chapman (London: R. Hart-Davis, 1955, 400 pp.).

Otto von Bismarck: a historical assessment. By Theodore Hamerow (Englewood, N. J.: D. C. Heath, 1962, 120 pp.).

Beethoven: his spiritual development. By J. W. N. Sullivan (N. Y.: Vintage, $1.

Wagner as Man and Artist. By Ernest Newman (N. Y.: Vintage, $1.65).

Green Universe; the Story of Alexander von Humboldt. By Edward F. Dolan (N. Dodd, Mead, 1959, 244 pp.).

Leopold Ranke, the Formative Years. By Theodore Von Laue (Princeton: Prince University Press, 1950, 230 pp.).

Hegel, a Re-examination. By J. N. Findlay (N. Y.: Macmillan, 1958, 372 pp.).

Nietzsche. By Walter Kaufman (N. Y.: Meridian, $1.65).

Karl Marx: his life and environment. By Isaiah Berlin (N. Y.: Oxford University Press, $1.50).

Mazzini: portrait of an exile. By Stringfellow Barr (N. Y.: Holt, 1935, 308 pp.).

Garibaldi. By Denis Mack Smith (N. Y.: Knopf, 1956, 207 pp.).

Cavour and the Unification of Italy. By Massimo Salvadori (N. Y.: Anvil, $1.25).

Tsar Nicholas I. By Constantin de Grunwald. (London: D. Saunders, 1954, 294 pp.).

Alexander II and the Modernization of Russia. By W. E. Mosse (London: English Universities Press, 1958, 191 pp.).

Leo Tolstoy. By Ernest Simmons. (N. Y.: Vintage Books, 2 vols., $1.45 each).

Dostoyevsky: his life and art. By Avrahm Yarmolinsky (N. Y.: Grove Press, $2.95).

Beloved Friend (Tschaikowsky). By Catherine D. Bowen and B. K. von Meck (Boston: Little, Brown, 1961, 484 pp.).

The Anarchist Prince: a biographical study of Peter Kropotkin. By George Woodcock (N. Y.: T. V. Boardman, 1950, 463 pp.).

Michael Bakunin. By E. H. Carr (N. Y.: Vintage Books, $1.45).

Franz Joseph I, the downfall of an empire. By Karl Tschuppik (N. Y.: Harcourt, Brace, 1930, 509 pp.).

Ibsen, the intellectual background. By Brian W. Downs (Cambridge: Cambridge University Press, 1946, 187 pp.).

Kierkegaard. By Walter Lowie. (N. Y.: Harper, 2 vols., $1.75, $1.95).

Lloyd-George. By Thomas Jones (Cambridge: Harvard University Press, 1951, 330 pp.).

Sir Winston Churchill. By Edgar Black (N. Y.: Monarch Books, 50 cents).

Hitler: a study in tyranny. By Alan Bullock. (N. Y.: Bantam, 95 cents).

Benito Mussolini. By Christopher Hibbert (London: Longmans, 1962, 367 pp.).

Lenin. By David Shub. N. Y.: Mentor, 50 cents).

Lenin. By Leon Trotsky (N. Y.: Putnam's, $1.25).

The Prophet Armed: Trotsky, 1879–1921. By Isaac Deutscher (N. Y.: Oxford University Press, 1945, 540 pp.).

The Prophet Unarmed: Trotsky, 1921–1929. By Isaac Deutscher (N. Y.: Oxford University Press, 1959, 490 pp.).

Stalin: a political biography. By Isaac Deutscher (N. Y.: Vintage Books, $1.65).

Three who made a Revolution. By Bertram Wolfe (Boston: Beacon, $2.25).

Rise of Khrushchev. By Myron Rush (Washington: Public Affairs Press, 1958, 116 pp.).

Ghost on Horseback: the incredible Atatürk (Kemal). By Ray Brock (N. Y.: Duell, Sloan and Pearce, 1954, 408 pp.).

John Maynard Keynes, economist and policy maker. By Seymour Harris (N. Y.: Scribner's, 1955, 234 pp.).

Benedetto Croce. By Gian Orsini (Carbondale: Southern Illinois University Press, 1961, 379 pp.).

Pareto. By Franz Borkenau (N. Y.: Wiley, 1936, 219 pp.).